Late 19th Century Furniture by Berkey & Gay

Brian L. Witherell

Schiffer Publishing Ltd

4880 Lower Valley Road, Atglen, PA 19310 USA

To my father

Key Words: furniture, Eastlake, Gothic Revival, Neo Grec, Grand Rapids, interior decoration,

Copyright © 1998 by Brian L. Witherell
Library of Congress Catalog Card Number: 98-85767

Designed by Bonnie M. Hensley
Typeset in Aldine 721 Lt Bt

ISBN: 0-7643-0656-1
Printed in China
1 2 3 4

Published by Schiffer Publishing Ltd.
4880 Lower Valley Road
Atglen, PA 19310
Phone: (610) 593-1777; Fax: (610) 593-2002
E-mail: Schifferbk@aol.com
Please write for a free catalog.
This book may be purchased from the publisher.
Please include $3.95 for shipping.

In Europe, Schiffer books are distributed by
Bushwood Books
6 Marksbury Avenue
Kew Gardens
Surrey TW9 4JF England
Phone: 44(0)181-392-8585; Fax: 44(0) 181-392-9876
E-mail: Bushwd@aol.com

Please try your bookstore first.

We are interested in hearing from authors
with book ideas on related subjects.

Acknowledgments

Special thanks to Carol Bluth, Amy Coes, Greg Kowels, Jay Anderson, Jerry Shepard, John Fornachon, Mr. and Mrs. Frank Boos, Debbie Dentoni, Joel Lefever, Ben and Ruth Mijuskovic, Carol Ziegler, Janet Long, Tina Boos, Ron Capek and David McCarron. Lastly, I would like to thank my parents, Chuck and Linda Steward, Angie and Brad Witherell, and my aka Mother Priscilla St. Germain for their unconditional personal and professional support.

Introduction

Through industrialization, a burgeoning frontier, and the use of natural resources, the Berkey & Gay furniture company became one of the leading nineteenth century furniture manufactories in America, with a showroom in New York and a vast wholesale trade through the Grand Rapids, Michigan, furniture mart.[1] Engaged in the Grand Rapids furniture trade from the late 1850s, the firm was incorporated by Julius Berkey and George W. Gay under the name Berkey & Gay Furniture Company in 1873.[2] The firm worked in a variety of styles, including Gothic Revival, Eastlake, and, as seen in the present catalogue, the Neo Grec. The Berkey & Gay Furniture Company exhibited and won a medal of the highest order of merit for two chamber suites in the Neo Grec style at the 1876 Philadelphia Centennial Exposition.[3] This recognition was a lofty achievement for any firm, especially a mid-western company on the cutting edge of the industrial revolution.

Pl. 1. Chest of drawers, 1875-1885. Walnut and burl, height 86" width 43" depth 21"; John Fornachon. Photograph courtesy J. Hill.

Pl. 2. Detail of drawer and stencil. Photograph courtesy J. Hill.

The City of Grand Rapids fostered several successful furniture operations during the second half of the nineteenth century, including: Nelson, Matter and Company; the Phoenix Furniture Company, and the Berkey & Gay Furniture Company.[4] Together, these firms formed the Grand Rapids furniture mart, an annual trade sale which attracted buyers from across the country.[5] The location of Grand Rapids, in southwest Michigan along the Grand River, was idyllic for this furniture trade. The forest of trees adjacent to the city provided soft and hardwood for the furniture manufactories while the Grand River allowed for the harnessing of power and the effortless transportation of materials and product.[6]

The completion of the transcontinental railroad in 1869, however, was perhaps the greatest asset to the Berkey & Gay firm. This railroad enabled the firm to export their furniture to various outlets in the continental nation, including the *nouveau riche* of the Pacific slope. One such outlet was the San Francisco firm of Wm. J. Heney and Company, a furniture company founded in the 1860s by Richard Heney, Sr., and his two sons, Richard Heney, Jr., and William J. Heney.[7] The association between the Berkey & Gay Furniture Company and Wm. J. Heney and Company is clearly demonstrated by the decorative relationship of a *Wm. J. Heney and Company* stenciled chest of drawers and a chest of drawers illustrated on page 17 of the Berkey & Gay Furniture Company catalogue. This correlation indicates the Wm. J. Heney and Company line of stylish and reliable furniture was imported from the Berkey & Gay firm. This hypothesis is further supported by the

Pl. 3. Chiffonier - Secretary, 1880-1890. Walnut, burl walnut, and cedar lined; height 72" width 30" depth 17"; private collection. Photograph courtesy J. Hill.

Pl. 4. Detail of drawer and stencil.
Photograph courtesy J. Hill.

unique drawer construction seen on the chest of drawers illustrated (in plate 2) and on a Heney stenciled chiffonier secretary illustrated (in plate 3). The drawers of both pieces are fastened with dowels rather than dovetails, a distinct feature used in the construction of Berkey & Gay furniture.

The intention of this publication is to allow for the attribution of nineteenth century furniture to the Berkey & Gay Furniture Company. In addition, this publication will expand the current knowledge of the nineteenth century import/export furniture trade and the craftsmen Julius Berkey and George W. Gay, men who came to personify the American dream through their ambition, determination and discipline. Finally, this publication will create an understanding and appreciation of this important era, manifesting the words of James M.

Barrie: *"Do not speak scornfully of the Victorian Age – there will be a time for meekness when you try to better it."*[8]

Footnotes
[1]Frank E. Ransom, *The City Built on Wood, A History of the Furniture Industry in Grand Rapids, Mich 1850-1950*, Ann Arbor, Mich.: Edwards Brothers, Inc., 1955, p. 22.
[2] Wilbert D. Nesbit, "The Story of Berkey & Gay - A Corporation which is Part of American History," *Munsey's Magazine*, September, 1911: 9.
[3]Ann G. Perry, *Renaissance Revival Victorain Furniture: An Exhibition at The Grand Rapids Art Museum, November 6 - December 6, 1976*, Grand Rapids, Mich.: The Grand Rapids Art Museum, 1976, p. 8.
[4]Ransom, p. 19.
[5]Ibid., p. 23.
[6]Ibid., p. 4.
[7]B. L. Witherell, *Witherell's Americana Auctions*, Elk Grove, Calif., September 28, 1996, lot 167.
[8]David Lavender, *California: A Place, A People, A Dream*, Oakland, Calif.; The Oakland Museum, 1986. p. 131.

Pl. 5. Berkey & Gay furniture showroom. Courtesy of the Public Museum of Grand Rapids, MI.

1880

Estimated values supplied are based on original finish with acceptable upholstery. When applicable, values were determined at unreserved general auction.

1. $4,000/6,000

2. $1,000/1,500 each

3. $1,000/1,500

4. $1,000/1,500

5. $1,000/1,500

6. $600/800

7. Left to right: $400/600, $800/1,200, $600/800

70 x 28

8. $2,000/3,000

9. $700/1,000 each

36 x 18

28 x 16

10. $400/600 each

11. Left to right: $600/800, $600/800, $800/1,200

13

12. $800/1,200

13. $800/1,200

14

14. $1,500/2,500
each

15. $800/1,200
each

15

16. Left to right: $1,000/1,500 $1,500/2,500

17. $3,000/5,000

18. $300/500 each

19. Left to right: $300/500, $400/600, $600/800

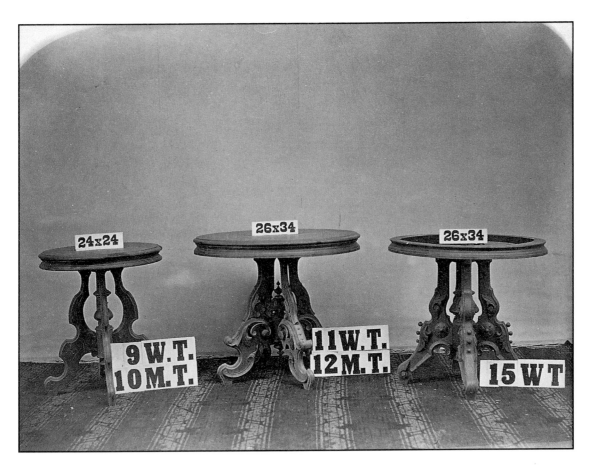

20. Left to right: $300/500, $800/1,200, $300/500

21. Left to right: $300/500, $600/800

19

22. $600/800 each

23. $80/120 each

24. $80/120 each

25. $100/150 each

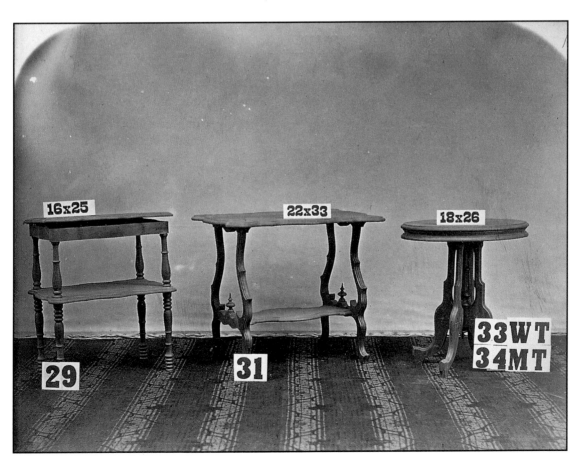

26. $200/300 each

27. $300/500 each

28. $1,500/2,500 each

29. Left to right: $100/150, $300/500

30. $300/500 each

31. Left to right: $300/500, $125/175, $800/1,200

32. Left to right: $800/1,200 each

33. Left to right: $400/600, $200/300

34. Left to right: $200/300, $700/1,000, $300/500

35. Left to right: $1,500/2,500, $1,200/1,600

36. $300/500 each

37. $300/500 each

38. $1,200/1,600 each

39. Left to right: $100/200, $100/200, $300/500, $300/500

40. Left to right: $100/200, $200/300, $300/400, $300/400

41. $2,000/3,000 each

42. Left to right: $300/500, $600/800

43. $700/1,000 each   44. $500/700 each

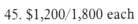

45. $1,200/1,800 each   46. Left to right: $150/250, $200/300

47. $125/175 each

48. $150/250 each

49. $150/250 each

50. Left to right: $100/150, $150/250, $200/300

51. Left to right: $125/175, $200/300, $200/300

52. With marble & mirror p. 60 set $1,200/1,800 each

53. With marble & mirror p. 61 set $1,500/2,500 each

54. With marble & mirror p. 62 set $2,000/3,000 each

55. With marble & mirror p. 63 set $2,000/3,000 each

56. Left to right: $100/150, 150/250, 200/300

57. N/A

58. N/A

39

59. N/A

60. N/A

61. N/A

62. N/A

63. N/A

64. N/A

65. $300/500 each

66. $500/700 each

67. $500/700 each

68. $600/800 each

69. $200/300 each

70. $200/300 each

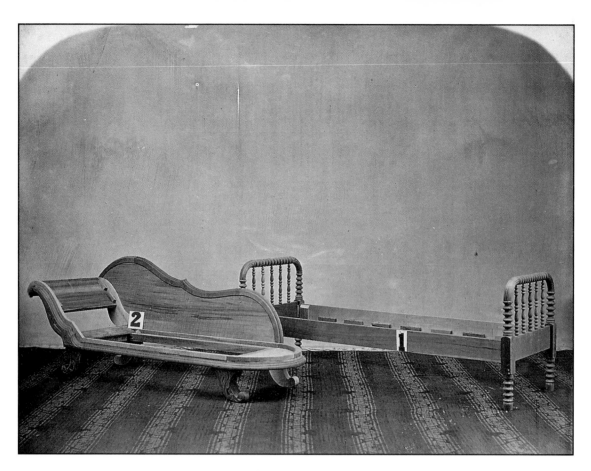

71. $100/150 each

72. $100/150 each

73. $300/500 each

74. Top left to right: $40/60, $60/80, $40/60, $80/120, $80/120, $80/120, $200/300, $200/300, $200/300, $100/150

75. Top left to right: $20/30, $150/250, $20/30, $40/60, $60/80, $80/120, $125/175

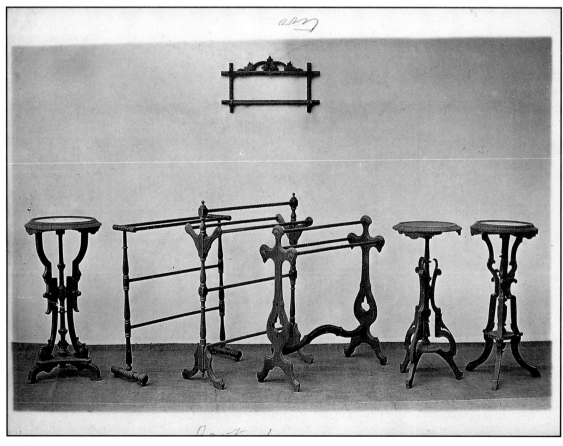

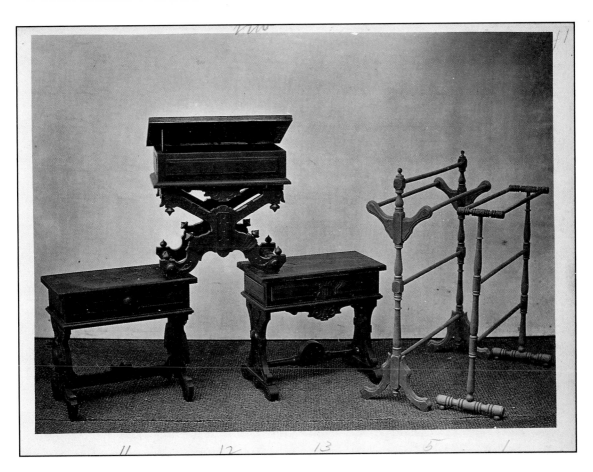

76. Top left to right: $150/250, $150/250, $150/250, $80/120, $60/80, $40/60

77. $800/1,200 set

78. With marble $600/800 each

79. With marble $600/800 each

80. $125/175

81. $150/250

82. $200/300

83. $300/500

84. $300/500

85. $300/500

86. $300/500

87. $300/500

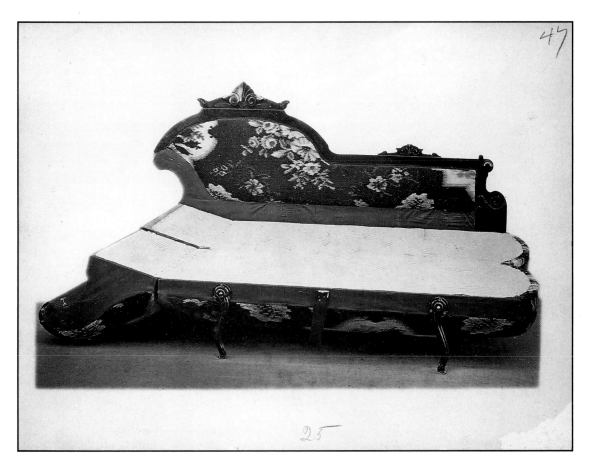

88. $400/600

89. $400/600

90. $400/600

91. $400/600

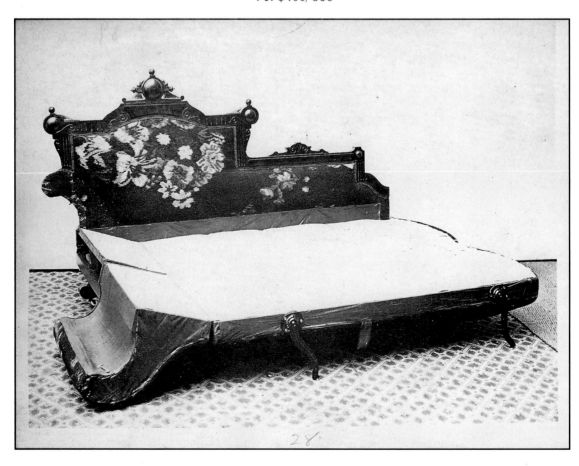

92. $300/500

93. $400/600

94. $2,000/3,000 set

95-96. $1,000/1,500 set

97-98. $1,000/1,500 set

99-100. $1,000/1,500 set

101-102. $1,200/1,600 set

103-104. $1,200/1,600 set

105-106. $1,400/1,600 set

107-108. $1,200/1,600 set

109-110. $1,200/1,600 set

111-112. $1,200/1,600 set

113-114. $1,200/1,600 set

68

115-116. $1,500/2,500 set

117-118. $800/1,200 set

119-120. $1,200/1,600 set

211

121-122. $1,000/1,500 set

211

123-124. $800/1,200 set

125-126. $1,000/1,500 set

218

127-128. $1,000/1,500 set

218

219

129-130. $600/800 set

131-132. $1,200/1,600 set

133-134. $1,000/1,500 set

135-136. $800/1,200 set

137. $200/300

138. Left to right: $150/250, $200/300, $200/300, $125/175

139. $300/500 each

140. $200/300 each

141. Left to right: $200/300, $100/150, $200/300

142. $100/150 each

143. $150/250 each

144. $250/350

145. $200/300 each

146. $30 each

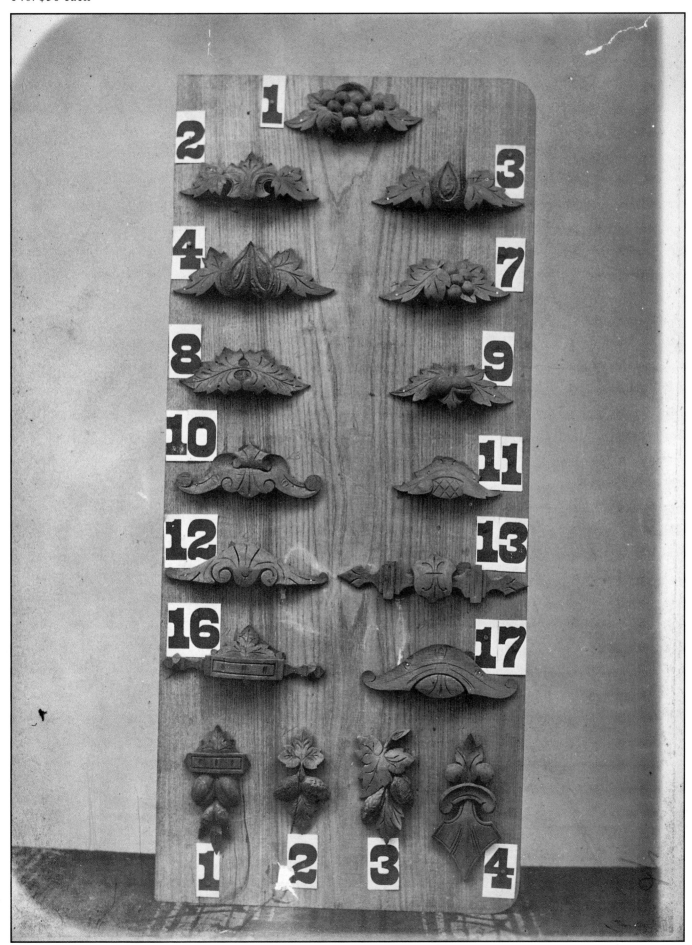

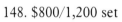

147. $800/1,200 set

148. $800/1,200 set

149. $1,200/1,600 set

150. $1,200/1,600 set

151. $1,200/1,600 set

152. $1,200/1,600 set

153. $2,000/3,000 set

154. $2,000/3,000 set

155. $3,000/5,000 set

156. $4,000/6,000 set

157 $4,000/6,000 set

158. $4,000/6,000 set

159. $5,000/7,000 set

160. $4,000/6,000 set

161. $4,000/6,000 set

162. $1,000/1,500 set

163. $1,200/1,600 set

164. $1,000/1,500 set

165. $7,000/10,000 set

166. $6,000/8,000 set

167. $5,000/7,000 set

168. $3,000/5,000

169. $3,000/5,000

170. $5,000/7,000 set

171. $3,000/5,000 set

172. $3,000/5,000 set

173. $3,000/5,000 set

174. $4,000/6,000 set

175. $4,000/6,000 set

176. $4,000/6,000 set

177. $4,000/6,000 set

178-179. $4,000/6,000 set

180-181. $4,000/6,000 set

182. $4,000/6,000 set

183. $4,000/6,000 set

184-185. $5,000/7,000 set

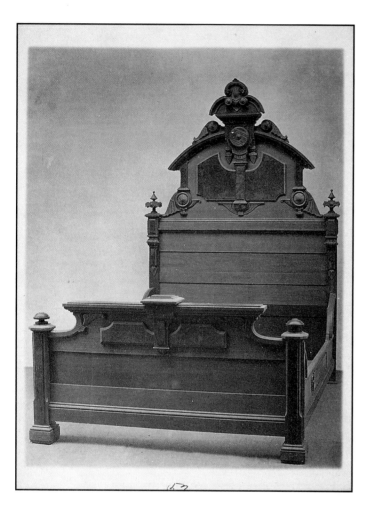 

186-187. $5,000/7,000 set

188-189. $4,000/6,000 set

190-191. $4,000/6,000 set

192. $800/1,200

193. $6,000/8,000 with marble set

194. $700/1,000 pair

195. $1,500/2,500 set

196. $1,500/2,500 set

197. $10,000/15,000 set

198. $4,000/6,000 set

199. $6,000/8,000 set

200. $4,000/6,000 set

201. $5,000/7,000 set

202. $5,000/7,000 set

203. $800/1,200 set

204. $600/800 set

116

205. $3,000/5,000 set

206. $4,000/6,000 set

117

207. $6,000/8,000 set

208. $2,000/3,000 set

209. $2,000/3,000 set

210. $5,000/7,000 set

211. $5,000/7,000 set

212. $5,000/7,000 set

213. $5,000/7,000 set

214. $5,000/7,000 set

215. $4,000/6,000 set

216. $4,000/6,000 set

217. $1,500/2,500 set

218. $4,000/6,000 set

219. $4,000/6,000 set

220. $5,000/7,000 set

221. $5,000/7,000 set

222. $6,000/8,000 set

223. $6,000/8,000

224. $6,000/8,000

225. $5,000/7,000 set

226. $6,000/8,000 set

227. $6,000/8,000 set

228. $4,000/6,000 set

229. $4,000/6,000 set

230. $5,000/7,000 set

231. $4,000/6,000 set

232. $4,000/6,000 set

233. $5,000/7,000 set

234-235. $5,000/7,000 set

236. $4,000/6,000 set

237. $6,000/8,000 set

238. $6,000/8,000 set

239. $6,000/8,000 set

240. $6,000/8,000 set

241. $6,000/8,000 set

242. $5,000/7,000 set

243. $3,000/4,000 set

244-245. $10,000/15,000 set

246. $5,000/7,000 set

247. $6,000/8,000 set

248. $6,000/8,000 set

249. $3,000/5,000 set

250-251. $8,000/12,000 set

252. $2,000/3,000

253. $2,000/3,000 set

254-255. $2,000/3,000 set

256-257. $4,000/6,000 set

258-259. $3,000/5,000 set

260-261. $6,000/8,000 set

262-263. $5,000/7,000 set

264-265. $5,000/7,000 set

266-267. $5,000/7,000 set

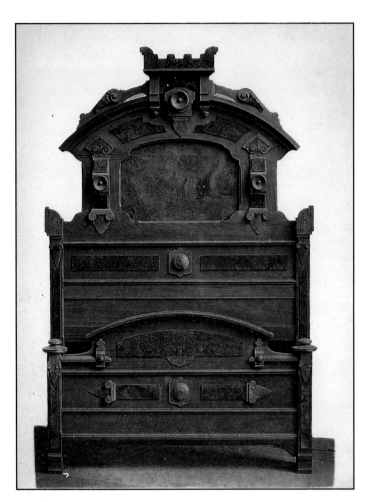 

268-269. $4,000/6,000 set

270-271. $3,000/5,000 set

272-273. $2,000/3,000 set

274-275. $6,000/8,000 set

276-277. $6,000/8,000 set

278. $5,000/7,000 set

279. $1,000/1,500 set

280. $5,000/7,000 set

46×30

281. $1,500/2,500 pair

282-283. $4,000/6,000 set

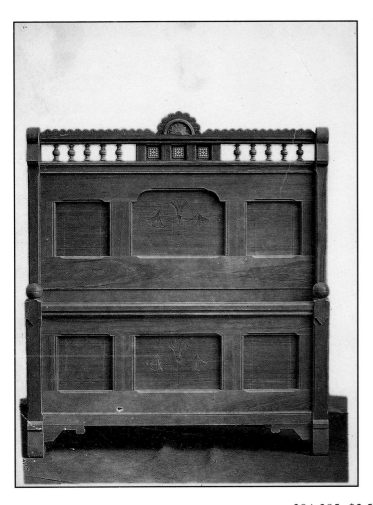 

284-285. $2,500/3,500 set

286-287. $5,000/7,000 set

288-289. $5,000/7,000 set

290-291. $3,000/5,000 set

292-293. $2,000/3,000 set

294-295. $4,000/6,000 set

296-297. $4,000/6,000 set

298-299. $5,000/7,000 set

300-301. $5,000/7,000 set

302-303. $3,000/5,000 set

304-305. $6,000/8,000 set

306-307. $6,000/8,000 set

308-309. $3,000/5,000 set

310-313. $8,000/12,000 set

314-315. $4,000/6,000 set

316-317. $4,000/6,000 set

318-319. $4,000/6,000 set

320-321. $4,000/6,000 set